Understanding The Divine Timing Of God

Understanding The Divine Timing Of
God All Rights Reserved

Copyright © 2015 by Victor Owusu-Teng

No part of this publication may be reproduced, stored in a retrieval system or transmitted in any way by any means, electronic, mechanical, photocopy, recording or otherwise, without the prior written permission of the author except as provided by USA copyright law.

All Bible references are taken from the New King James Version, unless otherwise stated.

Author's Contact: _vowusut@gmail.com_

The opinions expressed by the author are not necessarily those of Rehoboth House. Rehoboth House is committed to excellence in the printing and publishing industry.

EBook: 978-1-60796-900-6
Paperback: 978-0-9964267-3-2
Hardcover: 978-0-9964267-4-9

Published in the United States of America
by Rehoboth House, Chicago.
rehobothhouseonline.com

Table Of Contents

Acknowledgment..i-iii

Dedication..iv-v

Introduction..vi

Chapter 1
Understanding Divine Timing......................1-20

Chapter 2
The Prophetic Word....................................21-32

Chapter 3
Prophetic Restoration.................................33-39

Chapter 4
God's Agenda For You...............................41-50

Prayer of Salvation..51

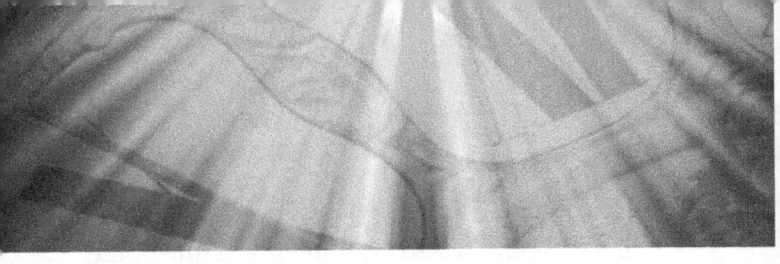

Acknowledgment

A spiritual treasure of this magnitude could not have been a reality without the collaboration of diverse gifts of some people I consider dear and special to me. It would be incomplete to publish such a work without acknowledging their time, dedication, talents and efforts that has helped me in this ministry.

Firstly, I thank my dear wife, Lady Gina, and our four children, Abigail, Aaron, Anna and Amy, for their patience during these years of ministry. Your kindness and patience with me both at home and ministry during the many days I wrote this book is greatly appreciated.

Secondly, I personally thank Rev. Dr. and Mrs. Stephen Gyermeh, the General Overseer of the

Acknowledgment

Church of the Living God Ministry International, for the support, contribution, inspiration, and indelible knowledge they invested and impacted my wife and I with. My heart is grateful. Daddy and mummy, words are not sufficient to express our profound gratitude to you for accepting us as your own children.

Thirdly, I thank Rev. Jesse Sackey and his wife, Mrs. Harriet Sackey, for their steadfast support and prayer for my family and ministry. If it had not been for your outstanding support and love, I would not have been able to devote myself entirely in ministry. My sincere thanks to you and your wife for standing with us faithfully at all times in ministry.

I also express my sincere thanks to Rev. Chinedum Brown and his wife, First Lady Patricia Brown for their resolute, steadfast, unwavering counseling and commitment in godly counseling. We shall be forever grateful to you Pastor and Mrs. Brown.

I wholeheartedly express my profound gratitude to Dr. Gabriel Amoateng for his godly and timely counsel. Thank you for giving us your valuable advice whenever needed.

Last but not the least, I express my deepest, heartfelt gratitude to Pastor Emeka Joshua Emeruem from Rehoboth House, Chicago, for graphically designing and formatting the entire book and also contributing immensely in editing it. I am proud of your work. Not only did you do a good job but also you did it with excellence. Thank you for the many hours that you invested in this work *"Understanding The Divine Timing of God."*

Dedication

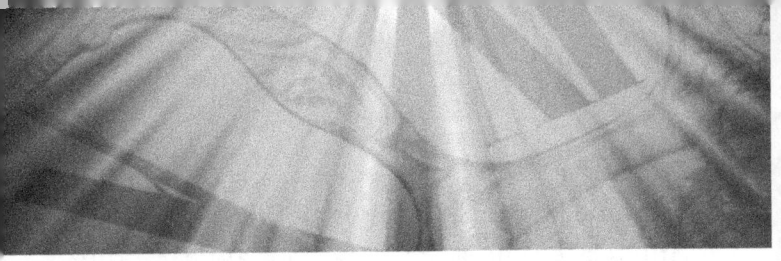

Dedication

With great pleasure I dedicate this book *"Understanding The Divine Timing of God"* to my dearly beloved wife; First Lady Georgina Owusu-Teng, who has stood side by side with me throughout this noble calling of God Almighty on my life. From the time the Lord brought us together as husband and wife some years ago, you have stood by me as my best friend, partner, advisor, counselor, greatest supporter, and most importantly, my closest co-worker in the ministry God committed to my stewardship.

You have been my faithful companion in ministry across the face of the earth more than we can reckon. Through it all, you have

Dedication

become an able minister of the gospel, an intercessor and a prayer warrior at heart. You are the most beautiful and previous gift that God has given me. I asked God for a wife and He gave me a lovely, virtuous, anointed, priceless, dependable, productive, practical, attentive, compassionate, submissive, hardworking, caring, loving, prudent and godly mother of our four children, for whom I have the greatest esteem and respect.

Thank you for responding to the call of God to take the Gospel of the Kingdom with me to the ends of the earth. Thank you for marrying me, for raising and nurturing with me, our blessed children, Abigail, Aaron, Anna and Amy. Thank you for being my comrade and partner in life and ministry. I am grateful and thankful to God that you will be with me until the end of our lives here on earth. Nobody is more important in my life than you. Thank you for everything you are and for all that you do.

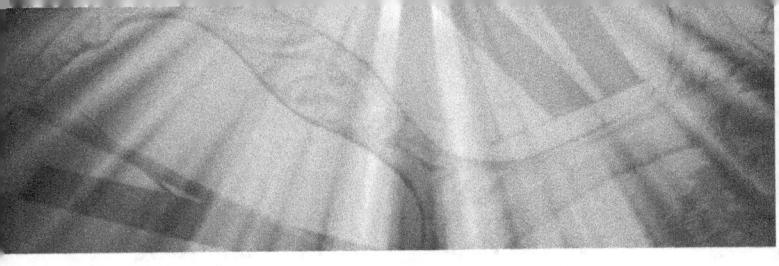

Introduction

The consequence of missing our time of God's visitation can be alarming. Some people have suffered stagnation, limitation, delay, denial, humiliation, shame, depression, disgrace and affliction in life for too long because they did not understand their time of divine visitation. If we do not understand God's timing for our lives, we will miss His visitation and suffer the dire consequence. God makes all things perfect at His time.

> *"Now as He drew near, He saw the city and wept over it, saying, "If you had known, even you, especially in this your day, the things that make for your peace! But now they are hidden from your eyes. For days will come upon you when your enemies will build an embankment*

> *around you, surround you and close you in on every side, and level you, and your children within you, to the ground; and they will not leave in you one stone upon another, because you did not know the time of your visitation" (Luke 19:41-44).*

Jesus literally wept over the Jews in Jerusalem because of the calamity that was bound to befall them. He explained in verse 44 of Luke 19 why they had to suffer such avoidable tragedy. You can agree with me that the consequence of missing our day of divine visitation can break the heart of God, even though He has provided us with every resources and opportunities required to avert such horrific experience. Consequently, we suffer needless tragedies in life. In Hosea chapter 4 verse 6, God said that *"My people perish for lack of knowledge."*

Job asked a profound question in Job 7:1.

> *"Is there not an appointed time to man upon earth? Are not his days also like the days of a hireling?"*

In other words, is there not an appointed time that God has set according to His calendar? To understand His divine timing is to understand His divine purpose in our lives in particular and for life in general. If we misunderstand the divine timing of God, we misunderstand His purpose for our lives. As the best teacher and wisest man that ever lived on earth; King Solomon, he reflected on the entire purpose of God for life in line with God's divine calendar, he concluded in Ecclesiastes 3.

> *"There's an opportune time to do things, a right time for everything on the earth: A right time for birth and another for death, A right time to plant and another to reap, A right time to kill and another to heal, A right time to destroy and another to construct, A right time to cry and another to laugh, A right time to lament and another to cheer, A right time to make love and another to abstain, A right time to embrace and another to part, A right time to search and another to count your losses, A right time to hold on and another to let go, A right time*

Introduction

> *to rip out and another to mend, A right time to shut up and another to speak up, A right time to love and another to hate, A right time to wage war and another to make peace. (Ecclesiastes 3:1-8) TMB*

Understanding divine timing will give you stability and control in the midst of the uncertainties of life. The Bible tells us that the sons of Issachar understood the timing of God. They had profound unction and anointing to reveal the timing and seasons of God. As a result they had control over the affairs of life and influenced the rest of the people. They literally walked in dominion because they knew what to do at any given time.

> *"Of the sons of Issachar who had understanding of the times, to know what Israel ought to do, their chiefs were two hundred; and all their brethren were at their command" (1 Chronicles 12:32).*

In other words, the sons of Issachar had unique anointing that helped and gave them understanding of the times. They were able to discern divine times; fortunes and occurrences. Fortune in this context means success, prosperity, estates, possessions and wealth. While occurrence means events, incidents, happenings, circumstances and their seasons. If we follow the Holy Spirit as they did, we will not only understand God's calendar, but also will know what the Body of Christ ought to do in this perverse and perplexed generation that is fast losing its bearing with God. The sons of Issachar, understood and had the ability that mentally separated, diligently distinguished and wisely dealt with the affairs of life at the time.

The sons of Issachar were those that did know. The Hebrew word translated "know" in this verse as "yada," means a revealed knowledge that comes from God, as opposed to natural knowledge that comes through observations from our five physical senses. It was a spiritual ability that the sons of Issachar modeled in Israel. The rest of the nation were aware of it and came to them for guidance. The Issachar's anointing has a good measure of spiritual discernment and revelation.

Introduction

Someone may ask how relevant the Issachar's anointing is today. Beyond any measure of doubt, it is as relevant today as it was in their days, because God is still the same and still works in times and seasons. To misunderstand God's timing is tantamount to misunderstanding God's ordained plan and purpose for your life.

> *"For I know the plans I have for you, says the Lord, 'plans for well-being and not for trouble, to give you a future and a hope" (Jeremiah 29:11). NIV*

God wants us to live by discernment and revelation knowledge, as opposed to head knowledge. It's difficult to exercise discernment if you always try to figure out things with your logic. If you're willing to say, "God, I can't figure this out, I'm trusting you to reveal the way out of this situation, then you can be calm in spite of not knowing the end result of the matter. Trusting God often requires not knowing how and when He will accomplish what needs to be done. We often say God is never late, but He isn't early either. Why? Because He uses times of waiting to stretch our faith in Him and to bring about the required change and growth in our lives. Certain rules of engagement have to change and align with the divine calendar of God.

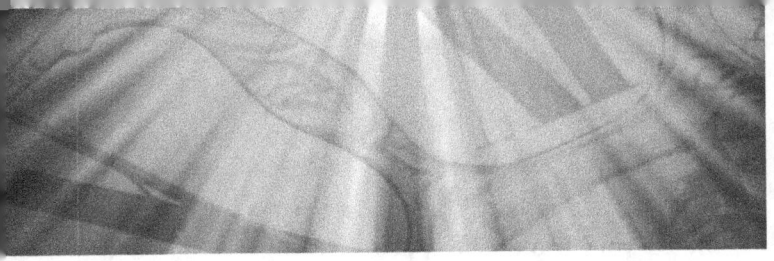

Chapter 1

Understanding Divine Timing

> *"He has made everything beautiful in its time. Also He has put eternity in their hearts, except that no one can find out the work that God does from beginning to end" (Eccl 3:11).*

Understanding the divine timing of God is necessary to live victoriously as a believer. It is a season set by God in His frame of time to intervene in our lives. If you understand God's divine timing, it gives you assurance that your seasons are coming, regardless of what your present situation is. The depth of that conviction enables you to see the end of the matter in God's perspective. I declare to you, though it appears nothing is happening at the moment, but at the fullness of time, the prophetic word God hanging over your life shall come to pass.

The children of Issachar understood the timing and seasons of God in their lives when others did not know the agenda of God for their lives. As a result they led and provided prophetic direction to the rest of the people in Israel.

> *"Of the sons of Issachar who had understanding of the times, to know what Israel ought to do, their chiefs were two hundred; and all their brethren were at their command" (1 Chronicles 12:32).*

I believe that when we understand this defining moment in our lives, it gives us rest and evokes unusual confidence in the Lord. It prevents us from unnecessary agitations towards others. It curbs unnecessary anger that could lead to increased blood pressure and suddenly turn our circumstances around for our favor.

Listen, do not cast away your confidence which has great recompense. God will surely perform His word concerning you.

> *"Then the Lord said to me, "You have seen well, for I am ready to perform My word" (Jeremiah 1:12).*

When Paul and Silas were in shackles as prisoners, they were able to sing praises to God. At that point, their lives seemingly came to a halt but their confidence in the Lord soared because they could see God at work at that turbulent moment. Ordinarily, they could have complained to God for not protecting them while doing His work. Instead, they lifted up their voices in praises and prayers to God. Their attitude attracted God's intervention in their case and the doors of the prison house were broken and the chains fell off their feet. They knew the timing of God and rejoiced in tribulations. Consequently, they came out victoriously.

> *"But at midnight Paul and Silas were praying and singing hymns to God, and the prisoners were listening to them.*

> ***Suddenly there was a great earthquake, so that the foundations of the prison were shaken; and immediately all the doors were opened and everyone's chains were loosed" (Acts 16:25-26).***

I don't know how down you may be but I can assure you that if you discern the timing of God, you can stand up and confront that situation squarely. You can look at the enemy and say, *"My enemy, do not gloat over me. I might be down today but the Lord is still my redeemer"*. I might be in darkness today but God is my light and my salvation."

In the midst of the uncertainties of life, you have to know the divine timing of God in your life. If you know it, when others are fretting and crying, you will be walking shoulder high and singing hallelujah to God. Knowing the divine timing will enable you to do great exploits for the kingdom.

> ***"… But the people who know their God shall be strong, and carry out great exploits" (Dan 11:32b).***

You might be down but you are not out of God's agenda. Therefore beloved, never be terrified by your adversaries. Remain resolute and immovable, always abounding in the work of the Lord. He knows your labor and all that you are doing for the kingdom. Your labor in God shall never be in vain. Don't be weary in well doing.

> *"So, my dear brothers and sisters, be strong and immovable. Always work enthusiastically for the Lord, for you know that nothing you do for the Lord is ever useless" (1 Corinthians 15:58). NLT*

David

While David was being hunted as a criminal by King Saul, he never allowed the life-threatening challenges arrayed against him to obscure his vision of divine timing. Though he was down, he knew he wasn't out of God's agenda.

Sometimes when you don't see the manifestation of God's timing in your life, it appears you have fallen down and out of sync with God. Ironically at such critical low moments of your life, you might be right at the top on God's priority list. In all his troubles, David still became the king of Israel at the appointed time.

> *"And there was war again: and David went out, and fought with the Philistines, and slew them with a great slaughter; and they fled from him. And the evil spirit from the LORD was upon Saul, as he sat in his house with his javelin in his hand: and David played with his hand. And Saul sought to smite David even to the wall with the javelin: but he slipped away out of Saul's presence, and he smote the javelin into the wall: and David fled, and escaped that night" (1 Sam 19:8-10).*

Elijah

Amazingly, after calling down fire from heaven and killing four hundred and fifty prophets of Baal on Mount Carmel, Elijah the man of God ran for his life because of Jezebel's threat to kill him. Though he was down but he was not out of God's agenda. God had to send an angel to feed him in his hiding place. There is nothing too hard for the Lord.

> *"And Ahab told Jezebel all that Elijah had done, also how he had executed all the prophets with the sword. Then Jezebel sent a messenger to Elijah, saying, "So let the gods do to me, and more also, if I do not make your life as the life of one of them by tomorrow about this time." And when he saw that, he arose and ran for his life, and went to Beersheba, which belongs to Judah, and left his servant there. But he himself went a day's journey into the wilderness, and came and sat down under a broom tree. And he prayed that he might die, and said, "It is enough! Now, LORD, take my life, for I am no better than my fathers! Then as he lay and slept under a broom tree, suddenly an angel touched him, and said to him, "Arise and eat." Then he looked, and there by his head was a cake baked on coals, and a jar of water. So he ate and drank, and lay down again. And the angel of the Lord came back the second time, and touched him, and said, "Arise and eat, because the journey is too great for you." So he arose, and ate and drank;*

> *and he went in the strength of that food forty days and forty nights as far as Horeb, the mountain of God" (1 Kings 19:1-8).*

Even at that lowest moment of his life, God was still involved in his life and ministry. It was this divine moment of encounter with the Lord that prepared Elijah for a glorious home coming and also received his last assignment to anoint three key people in ministry. Beloved, it's not over with you until God says it's over.

> *"The Lord said to him, "Go back the way you came, and go to the Desert of Damascus. When you get there, anoint Hazael king over Aram. Also, anoint Jehu son of Nimshi king over Israel, and anoint Elisha son of Shaphat from Abel Meholah to succeed you as prophet. Jehu will put to death any who escape the sword of Hazael, and Elisha will put to death any who escape the sword of Jehu" (1 Kings 19:15-17). NIV*

Esther

Esther defied the death sentence decreed by the king on anyone that enters his private chambers without his formal invitation. She put her life at stake because she understood God's timing of deliverance for her and her people. At that time it appeared Israel was down but not out of God's plan. Through Mordecai's intervention, Esther knew that she was strategically positioned in the palace at that time to facilitate the manifestation of God's visitation on Israel.

> *"Go, gather all the Jews who are present in Shushan, and fast for me; neither eat nor drink for three days, night or day. My maids and I will fast likewise. And so I will go to the king, which is against the law; and if I perish, I perish" (Esther 4:16).*

Her intervention saved the Jews who were under a death sentence and elevated Mordecai to the place of prominence in Shusham.

> *"When Haman saw that Mordecai would not kneel down or pay him honor,*

he was enraged. Yet having learned who Mordecai's people were, he scorned the idea of killing only Mordecai. Instead Haman looked for a way to destroy all Mordecai's people, the Jews, throughout the whole kingdom of Xerxes" (Esther 3:5-6). NIV

Zachariah and Elizabeth

Zachariah and Elizabeth were righteous and blameless before God, but Elizabeth was barren not knowing that God had set a time in His calendar to visit and make her an eternal reference point. She eventually became the channel through which God brought forth the forerunner of our glorious Messiah Jesus Christ. Bareness generally was considered as a sign of divine disfavor or judgment, and a social stigma among the Jewish people at that time. People could possibly have been framing all kinds of stories about them and making mockery of their condition. In spite of all the contradictions, Zachariah and Elizabeth were not out of God's plan.

At the time Elizabeth was barren, God was looking for a young virgin girl to incubate the messiah. Considering the age difference between Elizabeth and Mary, it's possible that Mary was not born when Elizabeth got married to Zechariah. According to God's prophetic calendar, Elizabeth was designed to bring forth John the Baptist as the forerunner for the coming Messiah.

> *"As it is written in the Prophets: Behold, I send my messenger before your face, who will prepare your way before you." 'The voice of one crying in the wilderness: 'Prepare the way of the Lord; Make His paths straight" (Mark 1:2-3).*

The divine timing of God can interconnect you with something in the mind of God that is not yet in existence. Divine timing is God's calendar that actually regulates what He has declared in eternity from His throne. It is His timetable through which He determines when to reveal His blueprints for our lives.

Mordecai

> *"That night the king could not sleep. So he told a servant to bring the official daily records, and they were read to the king. The records showed how Mordecai had informed him that Bigthana and Teresh, two of the king's eunuchs who guarded the entrance, had plotted a rebellion against King Xerxes. The king asked, "How did I reward and promote Mordecai for this?" The king's personal staff replied, "Nothing was done for him" (Esther 6:1-3). GWT*

Mordecai's scenario is a typical example of divine timing at work. When God began to move on his behalf, one night He took away sleep from the king and the king became restless. At that point King Xerxes decided to revisit the history books of his reign. Going through the chronicle of events, he realized that Mordecai had disclosed an assassination plot against his life by Bigthana and Teresh, two of his officers who guarded the doorway. They were actually the king's personal security personnel. Though the assassination conspiracy was consequently foiled by Mordecai's disclosure, but he was not acknowledged for being instrumental to saving the king's life. However, no one knew that God was working behind the scene waiting for the appointed time to come. At the fullness of God's time, Mordecai's acts of loyalty was eventually remembered and rewarded generously by the king because the divine timing of God for Mordecai has come.

Beloved, you may have been forgotten by men, but be rest assured that the good works you did for the Body of Christ and the brethren and continues to do can never be forgotten by God. Your moment of recognition is coming and you shall be celebrated at the appointed time. Remember, He makes all thing beautiful at His time. Like Mordecai, God is working behind the scene for you. Surely, your time shall come.

> *"He has made everything beautiful in its time. Also He has put eternity in their hearts, except that no one can find out the work that God does from beginning to end" (Eccl 3:11).*

We are living in a time when men's hearts are failing them as a result of the perplexities that have come upon many. Therefore, it is imperative that we understand God's timing in order not to be overwhelmed by the uncertainties of this generation we are living in.

> ***"Men's hearts failing them from fear and the expectation of those things which are coming on the earth, for the powers of the heavens will be shaken" (Luke 21:26).***

When you understand the dynamics of God's timing, where others fail, you succeed, where others fall, you walk through, where others are trapped you leap over and advance, where others are confused you know the right thing to do and move to the next level. Knowing God's timing will always give you an edge in life. The things that destroy people cannot destroy you because you know what others don't know.

If you are perplexed and don't know what tomorrow holds, I declare to you that though *"weeping may endure for a night but joy cometh to you in the morning."* You may be down today, your season will come and you shall be known and celebrated even by those that never knew you because the compelling glory of God coming on you cannot be hidden.

May be you are at the point where all natural hope is gone and you are asking, *"God, what is in this for me?"* Don't be despaired, God has put in your hands a life changing information in this book. He has connected you to a prophetic grace to cause a major shift in your life. I want to assure you that when you discern your divine timing, it gives you stability in the midst of chaos that is overwhelming others.

If you remain resolute in the word of God, you will not fall prey to the horror arrayed against many at this perilous times. Instead, you shall have rest in God like Paul and Silas who were praying and praising God during one of the darkest moments of their lives in ministry as discussed earlier.

Understanding Divine Timing

Your heart will not be short of praise even at the midnight hour of your life. Certainly, whenever praises and prayers are lifted high from a pure heart to God, His power comes down to inhabit such praises. God shows up in the praises of His children and empowers them to do exploits for the kingdom.

> ***"But you are holy, Enthroned in the praises of Israel" (Psalm 22:3).***

My prayer for you is to come to the point where you understand the divine timing of God for your life. You may be experiencing stagnation now, but know for certainty that your experience cannot alter heaven's agenda for your life. Just be still and know that He is God.

In the book of Job 7:1, the writer asks a question,

> ***"Is there not an appointed time to man upon earth? Are not his days also like the days of a hireling?"***

I declare to you that it doesn't matter what your situation is, God has set an appointed time of intervention for you. There is a time God earmarks for divine breakthroughs in our lives. At such times, answers from above becomes inevitable. If you get a hold of such times, you know without doubt that this is your season of divine intervention. It is like a pregnant woman due for delivery, no matter the oppositions and complications that may be present, she knows that her hour of delivery has come and nothing can stop that baby from coming forth.

You may be at the brink of your hour or you may still have some more time to arrive at your defining moment, it doesn't matter. What matters most is that there is an appointed time God has set for you.

> *"You will arise and have mercy on Zion; for the time to favor her, yes, the set time, has come" (Psalm 102:13).*

Understanding Divine Timing

Ecclesiastes 3 says that,

> *"To everything there is a season, A time for every purpose under heaven: A time to be born, And a time to die; A time to plant, And a time to pluck what is planted; A time to kill, And a time to heal; A time to break down, And a time to build up; A time to weep, And a time to laugh; A time to mourn, And a time to dance; A time to cast away stones, And a time to gather stones; A time to embrace, And a time to refrain from embracing; A time to gain, And a time to lose; A time to keep, And a time to throw away; A time to tear, And a time to sew; A time to keep silence, And a time to speak; A time to love, And a time to hate; A time of war, And a time of peace." Eccl 3:1-8*

I want to reassure you, if you know God's timing for your life, you will count whatever challenges you are going through at the moment as joy. If you understand the divine timing that God has appointed for you, it will calm your anxieties and take care of your worries. It will help you to remain faithful in your relationship with

God, even in the midst of storms and apparent hopelessness.

> *"My brethren, count it all joy when you fall into various trials, knowing that the testing of your faith produces patience. But let patience have its perfect work, that you may be perfect and complete, lacking nothing" (James 1:2-5).*

Understanding that God will turn your situation for better at His time, will help you remain faithful in everything you do. You will be faithful in your character, faithful in your marriage, faithful in your ministry and faithful in your giving. If you know and understand God's timing, whatever you do, you do with understanding and purpose as unto the Lord. Remember that if purpose is not understood, abuse becomes inevitable.

At This Point Pause and Pray

I come against every spirit of death.
I come against every spirit of disgrace.
I come against every spirit of stagnation.
I pray that I shall not die before my time.
I come against every spirit of shame upon me.
I pray that I shall not miss my divine visitation.
I pray that premature death will not be my portion.
Though I may be down, I declare today that I am not out of God's plan.
I declare that my end has not come. Until God declares my end, nothing can end my life. In Jesus' name. Amen.

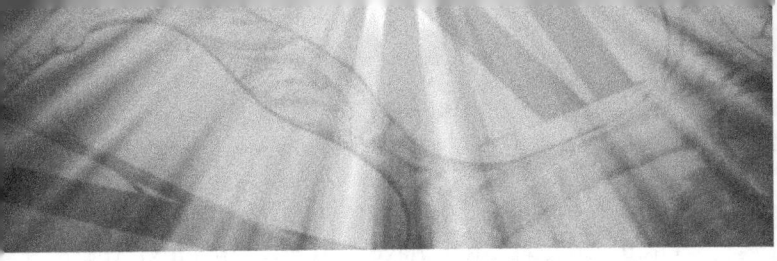

CHAPTER 2

The Prophetic Word

"Again He said to me, "Prophesy to these bones, and say to them, 'O dry bones, hear the word of the Lord! Thus says the Lord God to these bones: "Surely I will cause breath to enter into you, and you shall live. I will put sinews on you and bring flesh upon you, cover you with skin and put breath in you; and you shall live. Then you shall know that I am the Lord" (Ezekiel 37:4-6).

If there is any time to seek a prophetic word from the Lord, it is now. A prophetic word is a word from God that is spoken at a specific time when it is desperately needed. It's a word spoken in due season into our lives to confront circumstances that have hitherto dictated the pace of our lives contrary to God's will. It is a definitive word that is specifically directed to accomplish specific things in our lives. The question is, what does the prophetic word do? The prophetic word comes to restructure and reposition us for a better future. I can assure you, if you can discern when the prophetic word is spoken, you will know certainly that this is what you really need to advance to the next level in life and in your walk with the Lord.

It is a word that comes from God when we are at a crossroad in life. It may be a time when we are experiencing some setbacks, challenges and adversities or a time when we need a sure word to catapult us to the next phase in a particular area of our lives. At such times, these words become crucial to our survival.

I believe that God is preparing us for an unprecedented kingdom harvest. Regardless of what you may be going through now, the prophetic word of God can turn your destiny around and reshape your life for a better tomorrow. What God has declared into your life will come to pass because He has the ability and resources to fulfill it. Some people are easily overwhelmed by what people say about them that they lose touch with what heaven has written concerning them.

In the simplest form, the prophetic word is an inspired word from God that never fails. Sometimes the prophetic word comes when we are at the point of taking decisive steps in life, dangling like a pendulum not knowing what direction to go. The prophetic word can determine the outcome of our battles. It has the power to divide any red sea scenario in our lives.

"And it is easier for heaven and earth to pass away than for one tittle of the law to fail" (Luke 16:17).

The prophetic word is so precise and focused that it never misses target. One of the most precarious times in life is when we are overwhelmed by issues confronting and starring us at the face without knowing what to do. The nation of Israel was in a similar situation during the reign of King Jehoshaphat in 2 Chronicles 20. At this time, four enemy nations had aligned themselves against Jerusalem and besieged the people of God from all fronts. This scenario was a national tragedy with no possible clue to their safety. From all human indications, they were plunged into perpetual hopelessness and perplexity. At that point, the king realized that help can only come from God. He created an atmosphere for divine intervention by seeking the face of God in prayer and fasting.

> *"...O our God, will You not judge them? For we have no power against this great multitude that is coming against us; <u>nor do we know what to do</u>, but our eyes are upon You."*

See what happened from verse 14 after the king cried out to God that they have no human solution to tackle this problem. He told God that they were depending on Him to guide and guard them through this life-threatening situation.

"Then the Spirit of the Lord came upon Jahaziel the son of Zechariah, the son of Benaiah, the son of Jeiel, the son of Mattaniah, a Levite of the sons of Asaph, in the midst of the assembly. And he said, "Listen, all you of Judah and you inhabitants of Jerusalem, and you, King Jehoshaphat! Thus says the Lord to you: 'Do not be afraid nor dismayed because of this great multitude, for the battle is not yours, but God's" (Verse 14-15).

Someone reading this book might be in a resembling situation. I ask you today, can you turn that battle over to God and sincerely trust the Lord, the man of war, to see you through like He did to these people in Jerusalem? That battle you are fighting is not yours, as a result, you can't win it. Stop trying to do what you cannot and let the one who can, take the lead. What He did for one, He can do for another.

"You will not need to fight in this battle. Position yourselves, stand still and see the salvation of the Lord, who is with you, O Judah and Jerusalem!' Do not

fear or be dismayed; tomorrow go out against them, for the Lord is with you…" ***(Verse 17).***

It took a prophetic word from God to bring deliverance even at national level. I declare that a prophetic word from the Lord shall locate and settle any controversy in your life, in Jesus' name. Amen.

The Inspired Word

There is an inspired word of God for every situation in your life.

> *"For the vision is yet for an appointed time; But at the end it will speak, and it will not lie. Though it tarries, wait for it; because it will surely come, it will not tarry" (Habakkuk 2:3).*

There is an inspired word that can give life to anything representing death in your life.

> *"Most assuredly, I say to you, the hour is coming, and now is, when the dead will hear the voice of the Son of God; and those who hear will live" (John 5:25).*

There is an inspired word that can decide the outcome of your battles.

> *"Then the Spirit of the Lord came upon Jahaziel the son of Zechariah, the son of Benaiah, the son of Jeiel, the son of Mattaniah, a Levite of the sons of Asaph, in the midst of the assembly. And he said, "Listen, all you of Judah and you inhabitants of Jerusalem, and you, King Jehoshaphat! Thus says the Lord to you: 'Do not be afraid nor dismayed because of this great multitude, for the battle is not yours, but God's" (Chro. 20:14-15).*

There is a prophetic word that can deliver you from any kind of bondage.

> *"Inasmuch then as the children have partaken of flesh and blood, He Himself likewise shared in the same, that through death He might destroy him who had the power of death, that is, the devil, and release those who through fear of death were all their lifetime subject to bondage" (Hebrews 2:14-15).*

There is an inspired word that can restore your health and deliver you from any enemy of your soul.

> *"For I will restore health to you and heal you of your wounds,' says the Lord,'because they called you an outcast saying: "This is Zion; No one seeks her" (Jeremiah 30:17).*

There is an inspired word that can prosper you proportionately to your spiritual prosperity

> *"Beloved, I pray that you may prosper in all things and be in health, just as your soul prospers" (3John 2-4).*

There is an inspired word that can transform you from who you are now to another man or woman, like Saul.

> *"Then the Spirit of the Lord will come upon you, and you will prophesy with them and be turned into another man" (1 Sam 10:6-7).*

Every inspired word of God has the ability to cause change in any area of your life. It can affect your spouse, your children, your marriage, your academics, your career, your ministry, your finances, your health and your business. There is no limit to which it can impact. Apart from receiving an inspired or prophetic word from others, we can also begin to learn how to prophesy into our lives in proportion to our faith.

> *"Having then gifts differing according to the grace that is given to us, <u>let us use them: if prophecy, let us prophesy in proportion to our faith</u>" (Romans 12:6).*

The inspired or prophetic word enlightens our darkness, redirects our destinies, breaks any form of bondage and picks a man from the lowest position in life and lifts him to the highest position in life. That was what lifted Saul from being a donkey chaser to becoming the first king in Israel. The prophetic word picked David from the sheepfold and placed him on the throne as king of Israel. The prophetic word can never fail because God is not a man that easily changes his mind because of circumstances beyond his control. He has absolute ability to perform any word that goes out of His mouth.

> *"God is not a man, that He should lie, nor a son of man, that He should repent. Has He said, and will He not do? Or has He spoken, and will He not make it good?" (Numbers 23:19).*

The prophetic word of God is precise and sometimes concise. It comes with every accuracy like the stone of David that targeted and struck the forehead of Goliath in spite of all his protection. It does not miss target.

> *"For My thoughts are not your thoughts, nor are your ways My ways," says the Lord. "For as the heavens are higher than the earth, so are My ways higher than your ways, And My thoughts than your thoughts. "For as the rain comes down, and the snow from heaven, And do not return there, But water the earth, And make it bring forth and bud, That it may give seed to the sower And bread to the eater, So shall My word be that goes*

forth from My mouth; It shall not return to Me void, But it shall accomplish what I please, And it shall prosper in the thing for which I sent it" (Isa 55:8-11).

Unfortunately we are living in a time that many are confused and are finding it difficult to discern the genuine prophetic voice of God from other strange voices speaking purportedly for God. These strange voices are confusing many unguarded souls. Be diligent not to be caught up in the web of these strange voices.

I am encouraging you to biblically validate every prophetic word that anyone gives to you. If it is not consistent with the written word of God, discard it without giving it a second thought.

"I am astonished that you are so quickly deserting the one who called you by the grace of Christ and are turning to a different gospel, which is really no gospel at all. Evidently some people are throwing you into confusion and are trying to pervert the gospel of Christ.

But even if we or an angel from heaven should preach a gospel other than the one we preached to you, let him be eternally condemned!" (Gal 1:6-8) NIV

The Holy Spirit admonishes us to validate every word spoken to us with the written word of God. Any inspired or prophetic word of God must surely concur with the written word of God. This is one sure way to avoid deception.

As you read this book and diligently apply the unchanging word of God in your life, I guarantee you that your situation will turn around for better. God has put this message of understanding divine timing in my spirit to communicate to believers.

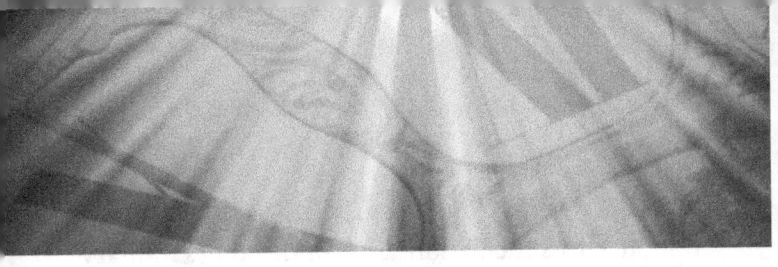

CHAPTER 3

Prophetic Restoration

"Hear the word of the Lord. Thus says the Lord: 'Tomorrow about this time a seah of fine flour shall be sold for a shekel, and two seahs of barley for a shekel, at the gate of Samaria.'" So an officer on whose hand the king leaned answered the man of God and said, "Look, if the Lord would make windows in heaven, could this thing be? "And he said, "In fact, you shall see it with your eyes, but you shall not eat of it...." (2 Kings 7:1-3)

When there was severe food crisis in Samaria, God sent a prophetic word through His servant Elisha and said, within twenty four hours there will be surplus food across the nation. One of the king's military commanders doubted and questioned the authenticity and possibility of the prophetic word. The prophet told him that he will see the word of the Lord come to pass but shall not partake of it. God in His infinite wisdom and power used four lepers to accomplish this prophetic word.

There were four lepers who always sat at the entrance of the city gate of Samaria begging for alms, possibly because of their social predicament. In the Old Testament, leprosy was considered an incurable disease. It was a social stigma for anyone to be a leper in Israel. The leper was considered a hopeless disaster, except God helps him.

After a while, these four lepers consulted and questioned themselves, ***"Why do we sit here until we die?*** They could neither go into the city of Samaria because there was famine in the land nor go beyond the gate, lest the Syrian army that besieged Samaria should kill them. After reflecting on their dilemma and questioning the next line of action, they decided to risk their lives and moved into the Syrian camp. Rather than lingering at the city gate of Samaria and die of starvation, they took the risk of survival and advanced towards the Syrian camp, peradventure the Syrian soldiers would spare their lives.

As they embarked on this life-threatening mission, God caused the Syrian army to hear the sound of a ferocious army rushing with horses and chariots towards their direction. When they heard the sound of an advancing army, they fled for safety and abandoned everything in their camp. The four lepers eventually came to the Syrian camp and were amazed that nobody was found in the camp. The dreaded Syrian army had fled and abandoned all their resources in their military camp. The four lepers were left alone with surplus of food, horses, chariots, clothing, silver, gold and so forth. After satisfying themselves with whatever they needed, they went to the city and informed the king that the Syrian army abandoned their camp and left everything intact. As the information spread across the city, immediately, the whole city converged at the Syrian camp in a stampede to take whatever each of them needed. At that point, the army commander who doubted the prophetic word was trampled to death by the rushing crowd.

> *"Then that officer had answered the man of God, and said, "Now look, if the Lord would make windows in heaven, could such a thing be? "And he had said, "In fact, you shall see it with your eyes, but you shall not eat of it." And so it happened to him, for the people trampled him in the gate, and he died."*
> *(2 Kings 7:19-20)*

God will always reveal to His prophets whatever He intends to do here on earth, not because He is limited in anyway but because He has the moral right and absolute ability to do whatever He wants done without revealing to any man. It is purely a divine privilege He extended to us. I rather believe that He chose to give us advanced notice because of His relationship with us.

> *"Surely the Lord God does nothing, Unless He reveals His secret to His servants the prophets." (Amos 3:7)*

The scenario in 2Kings 7 is one of such privileges as revealed by Prophet Amos in chapter 3. The prophetic word released by Elisha manifested according to God's timetable. We saw how the word of the Lord took hold of the hopeless situation in the nation and the king's commander who questioned the authenticity of the prophetic word. The commander's response to the prophetic word consequently determined his destiny.

How we respond to the prophetic word of God can either have a positive or negative consequence on our lives and destiny. In this army general's case, it was death. We have to be careful of how we respond to the prophetic word of God. God does not want us to cast away our confidence in Him, irrespective of the situation.

> *"Now the just shall live by faith; But if anyone draws back, my soul has no pleasure in him" (Hebrews 10:38).*

> *"Therefore do not cast away your confidence, which has great reward"* (Hebrews 10:35-36).

Regardless of your present situation, if you can act on the prophetic word in faith, there shall be a change. Nevertheless it lingers, wait for it. It shall surely come to fruition. Don't ever give up on the word of God. Faith demands actions. The four lepers acted in faith and brought deliverance to an entire nation. Let your faith cause a change beyond yourself.

When confronted with the storms of life, be resolute in your mind not to cast away your confidence in the prophetic word of God, regardless of the seemingly hopeless situation. At such critical times, refuse to take your eyes off from the unfailing promises of God. Naturally, you will be pressured to give up. Don't succumb to the pressures of doubt and fear of the unknown. Don't keep quite but continue to declare what God has said and silence the voices of fear and doubt. If God has given you a promise, it shall surely come to pass at His own time, though it may seem nothing is happening in real life situation, but behind the scene God is at work. Be rest assured that at the appropriate time, it shall be evident.

> *"The vision will still happen at the appointed time. It hurries toward its goal. It won't be a lie. If it's delayed, wait for it. It will certainly happen. It won't be late"* (Habakkuk 2:3).

God's Agenda For You

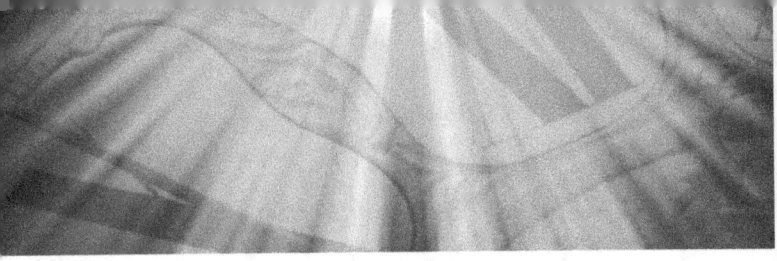

Chapter 4

God's Agenda for You

"For I know the thoughts that I think toward you, says the Lord, thoughts of peace and not of evil, to give you a future and a hope" (Jeremiah 29:11).

God's utmost desire is for every one of us to understand and fulfill His agenda for our lives. Irrespective of how fabulous and secured our plans are, God still has the best plans for us in every ramification. We have to come to the point where we allow and cooperate with Him to release His blue print for our lives, or else we shall struggle for a life time.

> *"We humans keep brainstorming options and plans, but God's purpose prevails" (Proverb 19:21). TMB*

The joy and utmost desire of any manufacturer is to see his product accomplish the purpose it was created for. It gives the manufacturer a sense of joy, significance and accomplishment. God is pleased when we align our lives with His agenda. Jesus said;

> *"And He who sent Me is with Me. The Father has not left Me alone, for I always do those things <u>that please Him</u>" (John 8:29).*

Regardless of where you are at the moment or what your experiences have been, God's agenda for your life remains intact. Though the Jewish people God was speaking to in Jeremiah 29:11, were still in captivity in a strange land at the time. Yet God reassured them of His plans of a better future for them.

Conversely, what God is saying to us is that our mistakes and battles of life cannot alter His agenda for our lives. It is our responsibility to understand what the agenda is and sincerely ask Him to help us experience it in our live-time.

When Saul was asked by his father to go and find a lost donkey, he never realized that God had visited him and opened a new chapter of his life. Prior to his encounter with Prophet Samuel, God had instructed his servant that, *"Tomorrow I will cause Saul to cross paths with you. He will be anointed the leader of my people, Israel."*

> ***"Now the LORD had told Samuel in his ear the day before Saul came, saying, Tomorrow about this time I will send you a man from the land of Benjamin, and you shall anoint him commander over My people Israel, that he may save My people from the hand of the Philistines; for I have looked upon My people, because their cry has come to Me" (1 Sam 9:15-16).***

Before we were even born, God had preordained a pathway for us to walk in while on earth and has arranged some destiny helpers to cross our paths. Understanding the dynamics of His divine timing will better position us to identify these destiny helpers and cause us to fulfill His agenda for our lives.

The Blessing of Obed-Edom

After God struck Uzzah dead for his error, the king and his leadership ran for their lives. Afterwards, King David found Obed-Edom the priest nobody knew of and brought the Ark to his house possibly as a setup, because he wasn't told that the Ark had just killed Uzzah. Obed-Edom was a worshiper of Jehovah in truth and in spirit. When the Ark needed somebody to carter for it, it was sent to his house. At times people could set you up not knowing that they are setting you up into God's agenda for your life that will lift you.

Please take your time and read the entire scripture. Don't skip it, I strongly advice.

> *"There was a man called Obed-Edom in the Bible, meaning Obed of Edom. The Bible says when King David wanted to get the Ark of God from the house of Abinadab, he invited all the priests*

but Obed-Edom was not invited. Obed means "Worshiper of Jehovah," so Edom means the black or the colored. He was a worshiper of Jehovah. The priest that the ark was resting in his house was called Abinadab. For forty years, he paid any attention to the Ark of God but did not give it the protocol and reverence that was required. Again David gathered all the choice men of Israel, thirty thousand. And David arose and went with all the people who were with him from Baale Judah to bring up from there the ark of God, whose name is called by the Name, the Lord of Hosts, who dwells between the cherubim. So they set the ark of God on a new cart, and brought it out of the house of Abinadab, which was on the hill; and Uzzah and Ahio, the sons of Abinadab, drove the new cart. And they brought it out of the house of Abinadab, which was on the hill, accompanying the ark of God; and Ahio went before the ark. Then David and all the house of Israel played music before the Lord on all kinds of instruments of fir- wood, on harps, on stringed instruments, on tambourines, on sistrums, and on cymbals. And when they came to Nachon's threshing floor, Uzzah put out his hand to the ark of God and took hold of it, for the oxen stumbled. Then the anger of the Lord was aroused against Uzzah, and God struck him there for his error; and he died there by the ark of God. And David became angry because of the Lord's outbreak against Uzzah; and he called the name of the place Perez Uzzah to this day" (2 Sam 6:1-8).

After three months that the Ark was in Obed-Edom's house, God visited him and everything within his realm of influence were immensely blessed. When the news filtered into town that God has blessed the household of Obed-Edom, King David came and moved the Ark out of his house to the City of David and placed it in the tabernacle he built for it. The blessing of Obed-Edom affected even his animals and changed the course of his entire life. His children were blessed, his business was blessed, his ministry was blessed, and everything and everybody connected to him were blessed beyond measure, just because of the abiding presence of God. Everything that somehow was linked to Obed-Edom experienced this contagious blessing. He was blessed to the point where he became an envy to kings and leaders. Prior to this time, nobody knew him.

When the Ark was killing people and needed to be given the dignity and reverence it deserved, Obed-Edom was the only one who could summon courage to do what was pleasing to God. Afterwards, God rewarded him immensely for that act of service to the King and His kingdom.

Nobody may know you today, but God sees your truthfulness. He sees your genuine worship in truth and in spirit like He saw in Obed-Edom.

I declare to you, your season will come. Your moment of manifestation will come and you shall be known by many because of the hand of the Lord that has come upon you. As you seek to do what pleases God, He will enviably reward your diligent service. Your life will be turned around to the point that people of nobility will be attracted to you.

> *"For God is not unjust to forget your work and labor of love which you have*

> ***shown toward His name, in that you have ministered to the saints, and do minister" (Hebrews 6:10)***

Receiving Divine Timing

We all want to experience good things in our lives. Unfortunately too often we want it now and if it doesn't happen as anticipated, we are tempted to ask, "when, God, when?" Most of us need to grow in trusting God instead of focusing on the "when" question. If you're lacking joy and peace, while waiting for God's intervention, it's an indication that you're not trusting Him as required. If there is anxiety in your mind and you feel worn out all the time, certainly you're not patient enough to trust God. Resolve in your heart to start trusting God like you've never done before, regardless of how bleak the situation may seem. See Jesus' advice in Luke 21.

> ***"By your patience possess your souls" (Luke 21:19)***.

The tendency to be anxious about the details of everything that's going on in our lives can be detrimental to our Christian walk and our health respectively. Sometimes it can be overwhelming and hurting.

Unfortunately I spent a large part of my life being impatient, frustrated and disappointed because there were issues of life I couldn't comprehend. God had to teach me to be less concerned with issues of life that I couldn't comprehend and stop attempting to know everything. Eventually, I finally learned to trust the One who knows all things and accepted the fact that some questions in life may never be answered till we meet face to face with Him in eternity. Refusing to worry over the issues of life is an indication that we have learned to trust God.

At times you may be asking, *"When shall my moment come? When will my season come?"* One of the reasons Jesus came is that we may have life and have it in abundance.

> *"The thief does not come except to steal, and to kill, and to destroy. I have come that they may have life, and that they may have it more abundantly" (John 10:10).*

The only person who has your appointed time is God. In order to understand God's agenda for your life and His timing, you have to draw near to Him and learn of Him. You have to obey His word and align your life with His infallible promises. You have to walk in absolute obedience to Him. As you consistently draw near to Him, you will begin to think like Him, talk like Him, act like Him, give like Him, love like Him, forgive like Him, endure like Him, and ultimately flourish like Him. Amen.

> ***"Draw near to God and He will draw near to you. Cleanse your hands, you sinners; and purify your hearts, you double-minded" (James 4:8).***

I may not know how this book got into your hands, but one thing I am assured of is that, God orchestrated the circumstances that brought it to you. Therefore, I encourage you to apply the principles enunciated in it with a resolute faith in your heart and watch to see the intervention of God in your life.

Prayer of Salvation

Peradventure you are not born again, I want to pray with you. Please pray along with me.

Father I thank you for giving me Jesus,

I believe that you raised Him from the dead,

I confess and accept Him as my Lord and Savior,

I believe that He is alive forevermore,

Thank you father for adopting me into your family, in Jesus' name. Amen.

If you prayed this prayer sincerely from your heart, I assure you that your are now a new person in Christ. I did exactly the same thing some years back and ever since, my life has not been the same, for better.

www.ingramcontent.com/pod-product-compliance
Lightning Source LLC
Chambersburg PA
CBHW052135010526
44113CB00036B/2264